A guide to almost

Fool-Proof Investor

By Gold D. Lion

While every precaution has been taken in the preparation of this book, the publisher assumes no responsibility for errors or omissions, or for damages resulting from the use of the information contained herein.

A GUIDE TO ALMOST FOOLPROOF INVESTING

First edition. March 14, 2024.

ISBN: 979-8224909278

Written by Gold D. Lion.

There is more to life than just money! Yes, exactly! So why do you continue to trade your life for money? If you are a new investor or thinking about becoming an investor in the stock market, it can be difficult to know where to start. Our school systems and our parents certainly did not do a great job preparing us to manage our money and invest it, so we can be financially free and retire on our terms. In this book, you will learn not only the mindset required to become wealthy. I will show you the changes I made in my life and what worked for me as an investor in the stock market. I compressed the most essential parts of my investing journey, saving you a lot of time and frustration trying to learn everything from trial and error on your own. How to budget and manage my financials, build a portfolio with index investing, and how to use a sector rotation strategy to maximise your gains. Without learning how to read charts or going through hours of research to decide what company to invest in. Although the name of the book includes the words foolproof. Nothing is foolproof! I try my best explaining my strategies and the steps I took to achieve my financial and investing goals. I am not you, nor can this book alone decide for you. You are responsible for your financial decisions. That being said, let's start.

Do you find yourself not getting what you truly want from life? You work, you spend money, and almost nothing is left by the end of the month. No matter how much you save, you will never be able to have the life you truly want. You work, you have an income, you spend your hard-earned money on paying bills, and have an expensive lifestyle you are not able to afford. Then the worst thing of all happens; you get into debt. What's left to do? Exactly, work more! Endlessly... for someone else until you are old with no savings, ending up begging someone else or the government for money to pay for you. If you find yourself in that situation, welcome to the rat race!

I am writing this book from your perspective. I want you to be able to steer your life in the direction you want, this is not a get-rich-quick scheme. This plan requires your patience. And the most important part of all, you will avoid the biggest regret in your life. When you're old and weak and cannot do anything anymore. You will regret that you did not live life to your fullest potential. Why waste more time watching TV, video games, and pointless relationships with people we don't want to spend the rest of our lives with. In this book, I will explain the steps and strategies I am using. Mainly what you do with your money passively. Meaning what you do with the budget that is available to you at the end of the month. Working on increasing the money that comes in through your own business and side hustles is for another book.

This is purely how you take your money and instead of spending it on depreciating non-productive assets and put your money into work with productive appreciating assets. The most basic way how rich people become rich is by putting their money into work. Almost like each dollar is a little worker of yours that can do work for you. Think about it, we, normal people see the rich with yachts, private jets, fancy clothes, and sports cars. Did you also notice that most people only see that side of the rich because that's what they would do with their money? Do you also see that that is the reason why they are broke?

There is a difference between rich and wealthy. What do the wealthy do before they are seen as rich? Before they put their money into the things that do not pay them back in any way other than look rich. They put their money into businesses, stocks, real-estate... everything that looks expensive for us... normal people at first but pays off in the long run. Let's say you buy a brand new car or fancy clothing because you want to impress your coworkers. After all, you want to look better than your peers. Or even worse a house to live in, thinking it is an investment!

You see, all these things are liabilities and nonproductive assets paying you nothing in the long run and only costing you money. What you want to do is look for opportunities to grow your wealth. Instead of buying all this nonsense you actually cannot afford without working until you die. You want to put your money into a share of a business your friend always wanted to do and now needs help. You put your money into shares of companies (stocks) you believe in and have strong fundamentals. You invest the money you have left into yourself to build your own business or at the very least to educate yourself about money. Which is what you are doing, otherwise you wouldn't be reading this right now.

Let's make a simple argument for the naysayers in investing. Everyone thinks they can save up enough money or thing's investing in the stock market is gambling. I want to ask them simple questions with a simple example. Let's say you have 10K and you want to save it somewhere. Take a hypothetical account you can put your money into. But now imagine I will take out 200-300$ every year and burn it in front of you. Some years (a year after a major crisis) that amount I burn will be higher, 700-1000$ that year. What would you do? Probably not put your money into that account, right? Here we go.

What if I told you, that is exactly what you are doing with your cash right now. Because of something called inflation. You see inflation eats into your pocket's purchasing power. The numbers on your bank account or the cash bill don't change yet the things you can buy with it does. Lowering the amount of money you have. Just leaving your money as cash or letting it rot away in cash in a money-saving bank account will not be enough to counter inflation and prevent your money from losing value.

It's time to learn about money and stop spending it on trivial things that neither are paying you any interest or do anything other than costing you your hard-earned money. It's time to take your life and cash into your own hands and put it into appreciating productive assets. You probably heard this sentence before: There is more to life than just money! Exactly, that is why you want to stop working for money and instead let money work for you. Giving you more time to do the important things in life. I don't want to elaborate too much on inflation, but you can view inflation as a way of taxing people without them knowing.

In my opinion that is fair since it is the closest thing to a flat tax, we can get in our current system. There are only so many ways a government can make money to pay for all kinds of free stuff people constantly want more of. A government can borrow money, cut spending(chuckle), it can tax or it can simply print money! By doing so the value of our currency slightly decreases while products and services increase in price. This is why your grandparent could buy an entire home for just 35K dollars while 35K today in most cases is not even enough for a simple downpayment.

While the purchasing power of your currency decreases and the prices of everything around you increases. The government benefits from higher tax revenue while your salary stays the same. Because wages are a trailing factor and take time to be adjusted and catch up with inflation. You have to figure out ways to hedge against that and take responsibility for your own life. If you don't, you will need to rely on the government, the coming generations, your parents... anyone else but yourself to catch you falling when you're old.

If you want to retire with your own money, you want to build wealth by investing your money into appreciating assets. You will not get there, by saving your hard-earned money in a bank that pays you a pathetic 1-3% interest rate that you are taxed on. You want to put your money into work. The stock market is an excellent option for exactly that. It is also an excellent hedge against inflation. Since stocks have a lower bar of entry. You can start saving your money with as little as $100 and expect an average return of 8-12% per year.

If you start with real estate on the other hand you need to save up a minimum of 10-30K for a down payment. With real estate, you have the advantage of leverage. But that is a completely different topic. If you start investing in the stock market you have one more advantage over many other investments such as liquidity. Liquidity is basically how accessible your money is to you in the form of cash. Stocks are more liquid than real estate since you can sell shares immediately with your smartphone and have them converted into cash.

You don't have to sell an entire apartment or home. A bank account is more liquid than stocks since you have direct access to it. And why is liquidity important? Because of emergencies. I know how you feel and I know in what position you find yourself. I know how it feels to have nothing, live out of a car, take a shower in the gym, and feel powerless. But I want you to understand that life is a struggle. The most badass people were created out of struggle. Just like a muscle you need to train. By doing so you break the fibers, it pains but that is the only way your muscles will grow stronger.

If you have a safe predictable and stable life until now, it will be hard for you to value freedom. The need for freedom does not come from a positive emotion as many might think. Rather out of fear, a fear of tyranny. If you feel enough pain you will adopt and value things in your life that lead towards freedom. And these things make you successful. Taking risks, being strong, and most importantly believing in yourself will set you free. You will make adjustments in your life and take the necessary steps to a better life. A life that takes you out of your current situation.

Unfortunately, our current system does not teach this to us. What we are taught as young children is to obey and do what we are told. To save for a secure life. To not go out of our comfort zone and out of our way to better our life to achieve the life we truly want. We are molded to believe in a fairytale. It is not true and does not correlate with reality. The fear to lose, the fear of the unknown, and the fear of being (different) standing out and being an outsider is a fear that has been installed in us from a young age.

You will swallow many red-pills throughout your life and learning about money and wealth is just one of them. The most important thing you need to understand is yourself. The market is the worst place to find out who you are. In this book, I want to show you the strategies and mindset that helped me achieve what I want to achieve. I want you to take this as a guide and be successful in your own way.

The most important thing that I needed to learn before trying anything was my mindset. Eliminating bad habits and taking the right steps in the right direction. Here are seven things people say who will never succeed.

1. I'll start tomorrow
2. I just don't have time
3. I don't know how to do that
4. It's just not fair
5. I can't do it
6. They just got lucky
7. It's not my fault

one: the best time to start is now. Whether that is writing the book you always wanted to write. Opening the business you always wanted to open and creating the things and working on the things that make you truly happy now. Most importantly starting to invest. Not on Monday, not tomorrow, now.

Two: You have to understand that most people fulfill their immediate needs. Their immediate desires. It is not logical and pure emotion. Living in a way only to fulfill your immediate desires is a recipe for failure and will make you feel depressed and less confident. Making excuses for the things that will make you grow as a person will not bring you far in life.

Three: I don't know how to do that, saying this is just an excuse for being lazy. If you don't know something and that thing is preventing you from your goal, learn it.

Four: It's just not fair is another way of deflecting responsibility. Weak people value Equality more than anything else because they are dependent on others to survive. I want you to value freedom more than anything else and that requires you to take your sh*** together and take some responsibility for your own life and become the best person you can become. Without relying on anyone for your survival. Do good things to become a good person. Build a business and employ people, give others opportunities. Let your friend sleep in your apartment while he/she is finding a new place to live or start over again. Offer money to someone you trust to build something they always wanted to build. By doing good things, you become good without even knowing it.

Five: I can't do it. Don't give up! Doing hard things is just building respect for yourself. That could be small things you do every day. Taking a cold shower, Sprinting as far as you can, or just writing 500 words every day will shape your good habits over time until they are not hard anymore and simply become who you are. Imagine a valley, you are standing on a cliff looking over the valley full of fog. You cannot see the ground or how far down it goes. Standing at that cliff looking over the valley is where you stand when you have an Idea. The greatest most elevated spot is where you are most motivated. That's where most people start. On the other side of the valley is a mountain, shining bright and gold in color from the sun shining on it. Between you and the highest spot in the foggy valley. You must go through that valley, there is no way around it. It is hard, It is painful And that's where most people give up. But the very few that make it out of the valley of fog and climb the mountain on the other side will be standing higher than anyone else shining bright like the sun itself. Doing hard things and doing them consistently will shape your character and that habit will eventually not be painful anymore and become who you are.

Six: Resenting the ones that have more than you is just another way of using inverse morality. You cannot just ignore the hardship and work that was put into creating something so good that people are willing to pay money for making the person you resent (better) than you. What Service or product are you working on or are you providing to attract people that are willingly giving you money to use that product or service? Unfortunately, many, unable to do anything useful themselves and are not willing to put in the work. Will twist the narrative in a way that makes them look virtuous and demonize the ones having more than them. Life is unfair and the world around you is neutral. You are born and then you die. How you perceive reality is completely up to you. You cannot change the circumstances you are born in but you can change the circumstances of your life by taking the right actions. Never say it's too hard or unfair. Come out of the valley as a winner.

Seven: Ahh responsibility, the kryptonite of many. If things go well they take credit and if things do not go well, it's not my fault! You are an adult and responsible for your life. Your circumstances are nobody's fault and all that counts is that you make most of what you have. Some people only make let's-plays and stream their gaming experience and they are happy. Think about that. I want you to understand that being successful in investing and building wealth for yourself and your family. Has less to do with how you start or with how much. It is more about you as a person. Your emotions and your habits and ultimately your lifestyle is the best indicator of your prospect towards wealth. Having 50K a year for some is amazing and for others a bad year. It's just a mindset. Imagine who you want to be in the future. What is the difference between you and who you want to be? It is not time as many might think. What separates you are skills and knowledge. You see that you want to have skills you do not possess yet. Get started on working towards becoming the best person you can be. It's never too late to start and time alone will not get you there. Investing is a mindset, do not invest the money you will need soon. Do not invest money you could use to get you out of debt. Do not gamble your retirement money with investments you do not understand. To help you understand investing in the stock market I want you to be familiar with a few terms. I am going to list them first and then go over them. Feel free to skip this section and get right into the juiciest parts. Even if you think you are knowledgeable enough I highly encourage you to go over these terms and concepts again. Here are some terms I believe you should know in and out before even thinking about putting your money into the stock market.

Compounding and compound interest

There is a famous story that explains the power of compounding perfectly. The inventor of the chess game went to the king. Showed him how to play and the king was so impressed by this man's invention that he wanted to reward him. The king spoke "Name your reward" and the man responded, "My Lord, I am a humble man who lived a humble life thus I only wish for this. Give me one grain of rice for the first square of the chessboard. Two for the next square, four for the next, and so on for all 64 squares. Each grain has double the number of grains as the square before". The king agreed and was amazed by the man's small reward. The king realized after a week or so that he could not fulfill the man's request, because on the sixty-fourth square the king would have to put more grains of rice than there was rice available in the whole kingdom. 18 quintillion grains to be exact which has 18 zeros and would weigh over 200 billion tons. That is the power of compounding. Here is another example. Imagine buying a pop machine, let's say it costs two dollars for one drink and the machine costs 100$ total. In one week (for example) you make 100$ and instead of wasting that 100$ extra you earned you buy a second machine! now you make the same 100$ by Thursday and at the end of the week, you buy two more machines. Now you get 4 in total and make the same money you made initially in a week by the end of Tuesday! you can do the same thing with your investments and shares you buy. Most brokers offer options for reinvesting dividends into shares automatically thus compounding it. That is called DRIP (Dividend reinvestment plan). You don't have to have a DRIP plan to compound your investments though. Just understand the concept. The Concept is the same for business and even life itself. If you have one coffeeshop and you want to open another one. Let's say that would take one year of work. The next one would only take half that time and before you realize it you are a chain and open multiple businesses per day all around the world. What you want to do is invest and hold long-term so your money has the chance to grow and compound over time. I would also write a journal for every investment you buy to keep track of why you bought it and for how long you plan to hold it. I highly recommend you to open up a compound interest calculator and set your goal. If you want to contribute 1k every month on a growth or interest rate of 8% and instead of taking out that money you leave it in the system and let it compound you would be a millionaire by the time you retire. Just because of the habit of investing periodically and the power of compound interest.

S&P 500

The S&P 500 is simply a stock market index of the largest 500 publicly traded companies in the US. Think of Amazon, Microsoft, Apple, etc...Wherever the country you are from have a look at large-cap growth companies that you can research and buy an ETF. Every country has something similar. The whole point is to later invest in the large-cap growth sector.

ETF

An ETF is a basket of stocks that you can purchase in one share. Instead of investing in individual companies (which I generally do not recommend), You can invest in ETFs that consist of several companies repackaged in a basket. That way you can Easier diversify and risk manage what your money is doing. You will also be able to sleep at night and go through several days without checking constantly on stocks and what your account is doing.

Index Fund

Index Funds are also ETFs but track a specific sector (Index) of the economy. They are also traded slightly differently than ETFs and most of them do not require active management thus making their fees extremely low. Just Like ETFs with Index funds, you will buy an array of Stocks repackaged in one, and more focused on the sector you want to diversify in. For example, you see that the economy is in a major downturn and to counter that the government lowers interest rates to encourage spending. Now you can ask yourself What Industries or sectors benefit from lower interest rates? Financials like banks and real estate are some examples. You can say with almost certainty that these two sectors will at least do better than the others in that phase of the economy. Now you can invest in indexes that focus on these sectors instead of buying shares in individual companies that are much riskier. And this way you don't have to do the same amount of work researching the ins and outs of a specific company. Because all you know is that that sector will be doing well and that is all you need to know. Later I will show you how I use index funds to build an entire portfolio and strategies on how you can diversify (without over-diversification) focusing your strength on specific sectors in a specific phase of the Business cycle. Confused? That's okay you will understand later.

What is a stock

A stock is simply partial ownership you can purchase in a company. When a company decides to go public, it makes some of its shares available to the public. Meaning now you and I can buy and sell shares in that company. Buy and sell stocks. For all naysayers telling you that's gambling. I have two questions. Do you think that workers in a company should be allowed to take some of the money they earn and contribute back into the business for the company to succeed? And do you think if that company succeeds those workers who contributed a portion of their hard-earned money should be compensated for their efforts? In the form of a profit share from the company? If the answer is yes, That's what stocks are! Stocks can be bought through a broker on stock exchanges.

Dollar-Cost Averaging and Lump Sum Investing

The simplest strategy you must know is called dollar-cost averaging. This means that you invest your money into the same investments in intervals (every month). and when an Investment loses value you simply buy more of that stock in a lump sum to lower the average. If you Invest 100$ in 10 shares and the value of your 10 shares drop to 50$. Most people would just sell at a loss... because they act emotionally and see what everyone else is doing. What you should be doing is to take advantage of the situation and buy 10 more shares now you own 20 shares for 150$. Of course, you have to make sure all the fundamentals are in line with your strategy. A bad investment is a bad investment no matter how much more you buy at a lower price. It is important to understand what you are investing in. You should only invest in things you understand. If the price goes back up to 100 you made 50$ or 25% on your investment by just being consistent. You buy and hold. If the price goes down you buy more. If the price goes up you buy less but you never stop buying a good investment.

Budgeting

'We buy things we don't need with money we don't have to impress people we don't like.' - Dave Ramsey

Before getting excited about investing and aimlessly throwing your hard-earned money into things you don't understand. It is very important that you first understand money and get your budgeting right. I will show you a budgeting plan that will help you get into investing and a method on how to invest periodically. This plan is an extension of the 50 / 30 / 20 Rule. This rule is basically that you use 50% of your money to pay for necessities. 30% towards your wants and things that are not necessary and 20% goes towards your savings (investments)

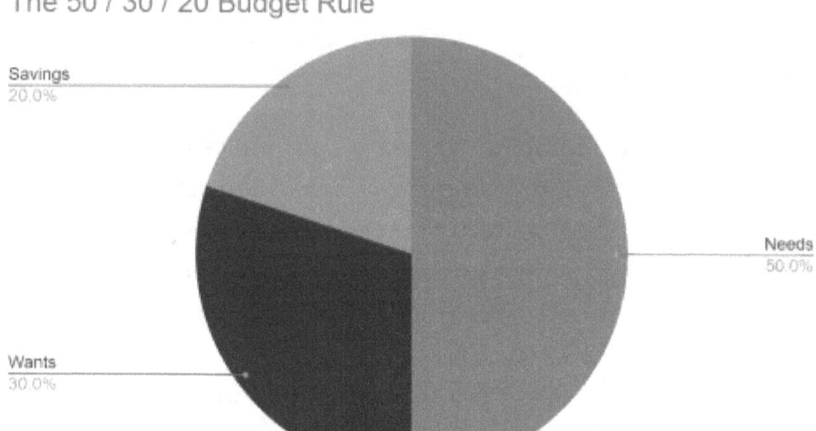

In my opinion, also the opinion of many successful people talking about this topic. You should be able to invest/Save 30% of your total budget and try to live frugally below your means. Ideally with just half so 50% of your monthly income. The biggest money drain is when people live a lifestyle that is well above their means and the worst part is that many cannot maintain their lifestyle realistically and end up going into a lot of depts. This could happen as easily as just getting a 20-40K student loan and then spending that money on a new car, partying, etc... Until the money runs out.

Live below your means and maintain a lifestyle you can afford. This plan includes a 10% allocation towards an emergency fund and a 15% towards a dream account. If you already have an emergency fund, that's great! You can dedicate more of your money towards saving and investing. For the dream account and others, you could tweak the numbers to what suits your strategy best. Try to invest and save a minimum of 25-30% of your income.

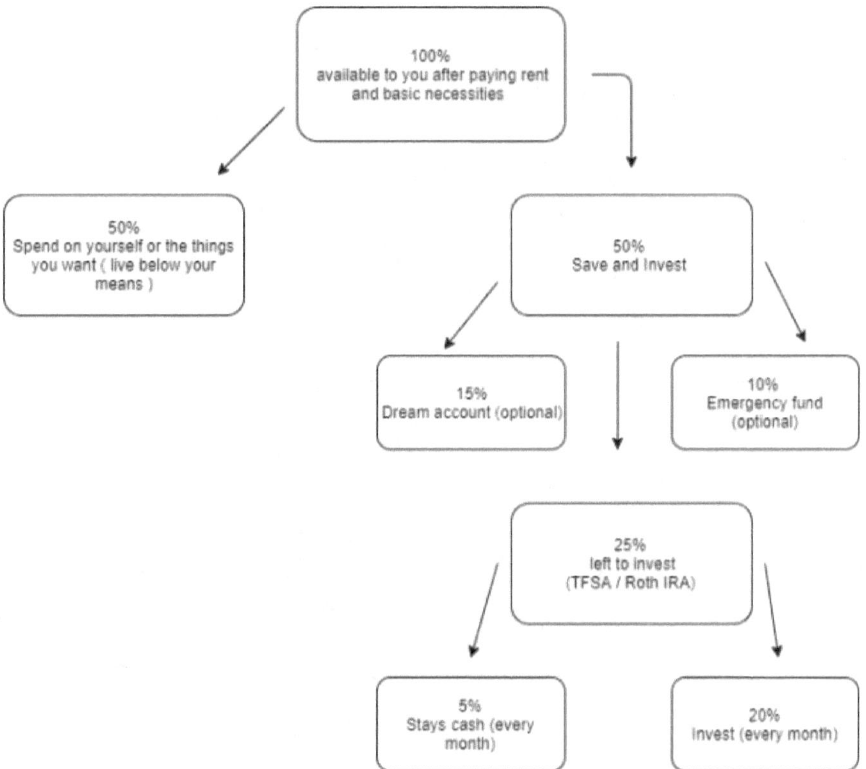

In this Illustration, you start with 100% assuming you paid your most necessities mainly rent hydro and your car bills. Then you use 50% of that to spend on the things you want and the other 50% you set aside to save and invest. After paying for your necessities you are left with 2000$ every month. 1000$ you use for clothes, hobbies, your partner whatever. I would even argue groceries despite many calling it a necessity. I'd say it is something in between, since you are left with a choice. You don't have to eat organic. you don't have to eat out. You don't have to buy snacks, soda, and alcohol. Think about what you really do need and adjust accordingly. The other 1000$ you put aside to save and invest. Assuming you do not have an emergency fund or are in the process of building an emergency fund. Having one should be your number one priority right after paying off your debt. The final budgeting plan for investing should look something like this (with an example of 1000$ available to you every month):

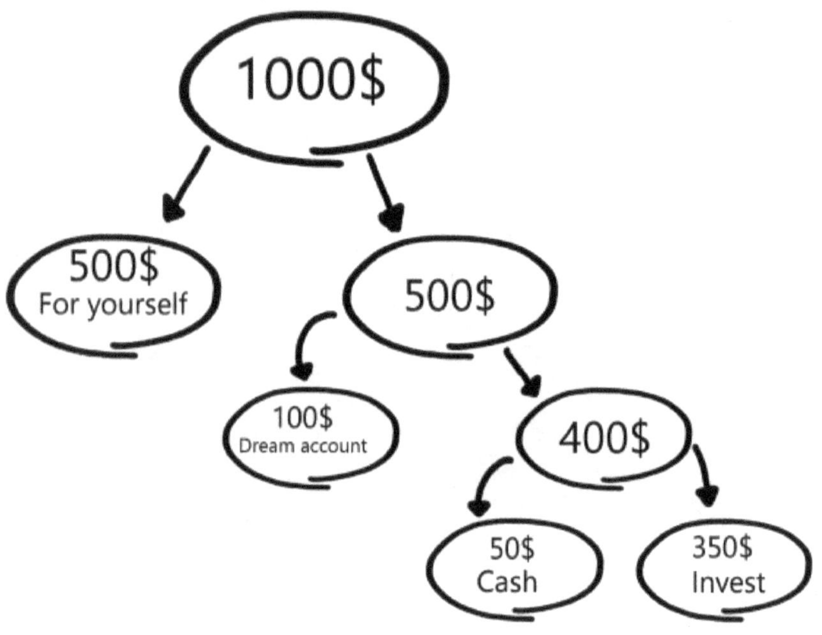

After only one year of doing this every month your budget would look something like this:

4200$ invested

600$ cash (in investing account)

1200$ in your dream account

This is the result of a simple habit you repeat every month... Amazing!

Let's use some illustrations to show how you manage the cash in your investing account with a dollar-cost averaging and lump sum investing strategy:

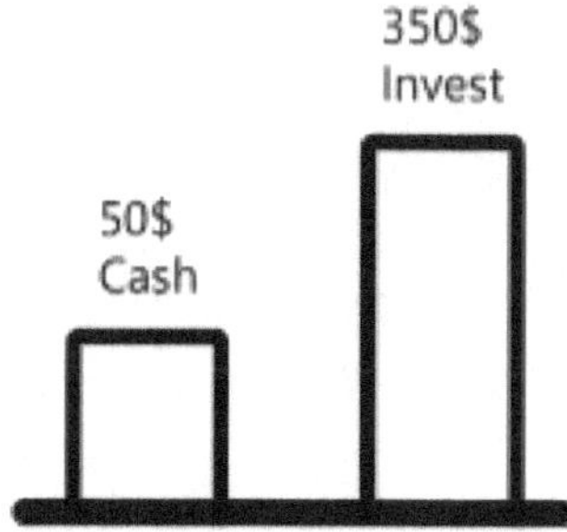

This is how your investing budget looks like every month with markets largely unchanged.

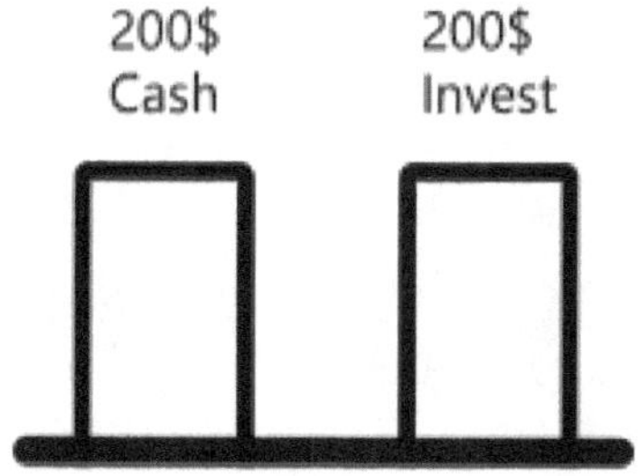

This is for the months where the markets are overvalued. Your grandpa is talking about the latest penny stock he invested in and your neighbor Kevin just bought his first bitcoin. The peak of a bull market.

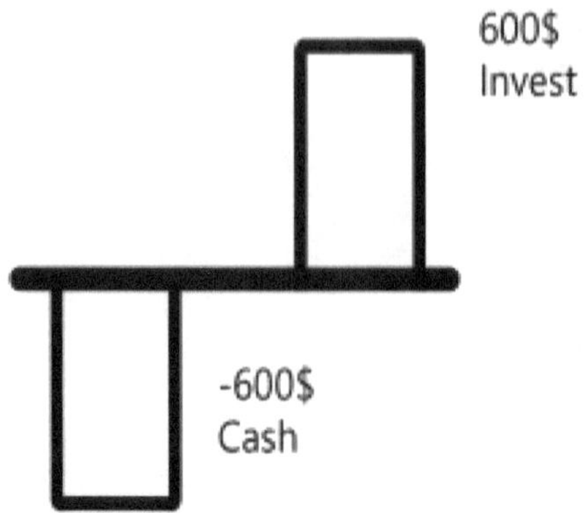

This is a correction or a full-on market crash. The moment you have been waiting for to finally deploy the cash you accumulated on the side over the months and years. Markets are mostly red and in these months you use the cash you kept on the sidelines to take advantage of low prices and assets that are now on a massive discount.

Emergency Fund

10% or 100$ should go towards your emergency fund assuming you don't have one yet or you are in the process of building one. Or you do have one but you took out money to pay for something urgent that came up. Your emergency fund should be 6 months of your monthly expenses on the side in cash. In case you are laid off from work. Or something urgent comes up and you need money. In our example that would be 2000$*6=12000$ or 6000$ assuming a 1000$ monthly living expense as a bare minimum. Before investing and saving up money, you should work to have cash ready as your emergency fund in a high-interest paying savings account. It has to be Liquid and accessible to you immediately. This way you can take a loan from yourself and pay it back to yourself in case of an emergency. You don't have to take a loan and go into debt or beg someone for money when it's too late. If you already have your emergency fund, that's great. now you can allocate more towards investing.

Dream Account

15% of your savings every month should go into what I call a dream Account. Just like with the emergency fund you want to be able to take a loan from yourself in case an opportunity arises. That way you will have money for trying a new business idea or helping a friend with their business. Or for a down payment of a property. This is the money that you have on the side so that you are ready for any opportunity that comes your way. You could hold this fund in cash on a bank account or put it into a low-risk liquid asset. Liquidity is key, because opportunities come and go fast and you want your money to be accessible as fast as possible.

What you invest

Now you are left with 25% or 500$ that you can invest. I would still say that this should be around 30% which would be without the 10% emergency fund so get that out of the way first. Once you set up your emergency fund especially if you are young. Do not save, invest everything. Compounding is most powerful when given time. The best time to start is now and the earlier you start the more your money can compound.

If you are Canadian, start by opening a self-directed tax-free savings account or TFSA in short and/or setting up an individual RRSP account. You can set up a retirement plan with your employer as well. In the US that would be your Roth IRA and 401K that you can also set up with your employer. Both can be used to invest. Wherever you are from, I would do my research and seek opportunities available in your country.

In Canada and the US, The TFSA / Roth IRA are tax-exempt up to a certain amount with an allowed contribution room every year. With an RRSP / 401K your contribution towards these accounts is tax-deferred, meaning you will pay taxes when you withdraw money. I would research and find something similar in the country you are living in. Once opened with an online broker or your bank, don't just pay into your account and let cash accumulate there. The idea is that you put your money into work. In this example leave 5% cash and invest 20% and the ratio between how much stays cash and how much is invested every month depends on your strategy which I will discuss in more detail later. What you invest and how you invest depends on you as a person. Age, income, and risk tolerance are just a few of the many factors that will influence how you will invest. If you are lazy and don't want to spend endless hours on what company is best to put your money in. That is not necessarily a negative thing. I would suggest an easy Mutual fund that you can either set up with your bank or online broker. At the same time Invest or start only investing into a low fee index fund with a good history of stable returns. The easiest would be an Index ETF that tracks the S&P 500 US index. If you are from Canada, you can find US ETFs that are offered in Canadian Dollars.

An index fund that tracks the S&P 500 is tracking the top performing 500 companies in the US in Canadian dollars. If you have a mutual fund and an index fund at the same time you can compare the two and how they perform. If your mutual fund outperforms the Index fund. It might be worth paying the extra fee to the fund manager. Since you will save a lot of time and headache searching and investing by yourself. However, doing it by yourself is not as difficult as it seems. If your Index performs better than the mutual fund it's time to fire your manager and put a little effort into yourself to maximize your investment gains. We will go over maximizing your index investing later. Let's say you decide to continue investing in your index fund and want to build a portfolio with stocks or ETFs of your choice. I mention that 5% stay in cash each month. The idea is that you invest periodically every month into your portfolio.

If your investments have been down for a while you might consider simply investing the full amount or 25% that period and not put aside any cash. Since now all the investments you spend money on are for a discount. If your investments have been green and up for a while maybe you want to lower the % of how much you invest to 10-15% and save more cash 10%. The cash that you accumulate over time each period is there so you have enough on the side when everything is on a discount.

Just like with your dream account, you want to be able to use the opportunity to invest when there is a downturn in the market. We saw what happened with the coronavirus: all major stocks went down by 50% meaning you could buy for half price! And the recovery brought insane gains to people. You don't want to miss out on massive opportunities like these. At least have 5% in cash available and if you have a very aggressive portfolio you might consider having 20-30%cash ready at any given time.

The formula to lose weight is simple. Take in fewer calories than you burn. That's it. The key is to be in a calorie deficit and that's the formula to losing weight. How you do it and your strategy is up to you. Whether going on a keto diet, intermittent fasting or becoming vegan are all just strategies you use to reach the same goal. It is the same for becoming wealthy. The formula is simple, Increase cash flow and invest into appreciating productive assets. Increasing cash flow through opening a business or combining it with an investment like real estate.

Investing in the stock market is just a means to reach the same goal. Just like with losing weight, creating wealth from scratch is a process that requires your lifestyle to change. You will need patience and have to be persistent to reach your goal. Money is just a means, the goal is your freedom. The freedom to do what you want with your own time especially not trading in your time for money. To gain freedom in your life you have to take responsibility for your life. Because freedom and responsibility go hand in hand. Make the necessary changes in your life that will lead you towards your goal. Get rid of bad habits and focus on what you want from life. There are some beliefs and habits that helped me enormously in my own life. Looking back and comparing myself to myself in the past and how much I improved as a person makes me extremely happy. We should stop comparing ourselves to others and start comparing ourselves to ourselves.

The secret is to keep going and keep trying new things because every challenge you take requires you to think and learn new skills and develop strategies that give you the ability to tackle more ambitious goals. Who knows where those new abilities will take you. On the next page are some habits I changed to improve myself as a person.

Preparation

When you wake up and look at your phone to go through social media and see what is new remember you already made a mistake. Plan your day. Do that at least the night before setting mini-goals you can achieve. I will Finnish this project today, I will make my website, I will walk to work. These little habits you will do will eventually become you and set you free to a greater you. Try to do difficult things every day, even if it's just a cold shower. It builds respect for yourself.

Structure

not only plan but structure your life, do not do what you feel like at the moment do not be a slave of your desires, you wake up each day the same time you make and eat breakfast every day you go to the gym every day you have a routine ...every .... day. You do a certain thing enough time until you do not think about it anymore it became a habit structure and planning will eventually set you free from your slavery.

Feel failure

Sometimes you are sad you can't Finnish what you wanted you had a crappy day at work and some people make you feel you are a failure. Do not make the mistake and try to suppress your feelings (oh I'm not sad, oh things are not really bad) no. You have to remember it is okay to feel sad sometimes. it is okay to fail it is okay to be depressed you have to feel your emotions do not detach yourself from yourself. You have to know what is happening inside of you only this way you will find yourself.

Seek internal and not external validation

Remember to not be a slave of your desires? You want to impress this girl or you want to make others proud, you want to be the funniest or coolest person you want to strengthen your image, how others see you, is not who you are. You gotta reflect on yourself and look inside of you who you are. What do you love, what makes you proud of yourself, remind yourself of these things and seek internal validation. Do not be a slave of how others see you it is not you.

No one owes you anything and you don't owe anyone anything either

Not your parents, your brother, your sister, your lover anyone. As selfish as it might sound your happiness and your life comes first. You don't live for anybody but yourself. What do you love, what do you do, what do you fight for and what would you sacrifice? Ask yourself these things and be the best you can be.

Building a Portfolio

Building a decent portfolio is probably the first thing you want to consider when investing. Every portfolio is different and differs from person to person. Mainly it is all about your risk tolerance. High risk means high returns, while low risk gives you low returns. Let's say your portfolio's 10-year average is 10% that doesn't mean you earned 10% every year, one year you made -40% the other year +20 understand that all this is due to volatility. A Conservative portfolio has less return but is also less volatile. For a stable conservative portfolio investments are largely Large-cap value stocks that pay good dividends. Or consist mainly of bonds.

Typical conservative portfolio:

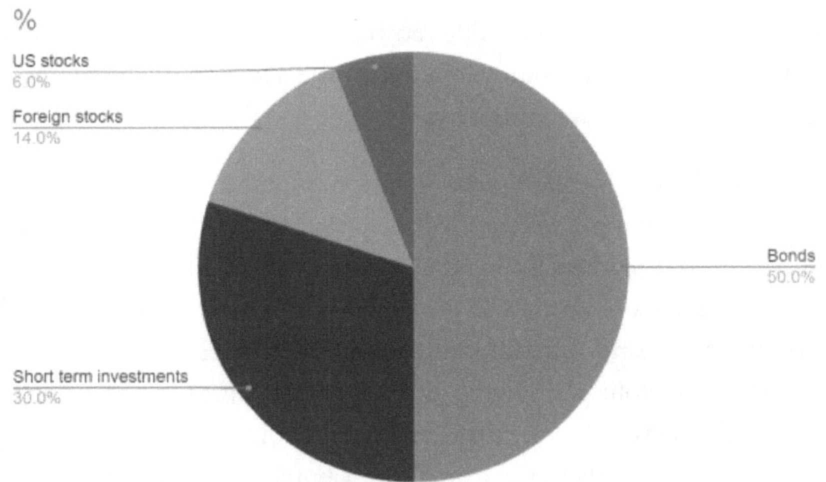

An aggressive portfolio has higher returns but is also more volatile. An aggressive portfolio mainly consisting of stocks, is less diversified and more concentrated on specific growth stocks:

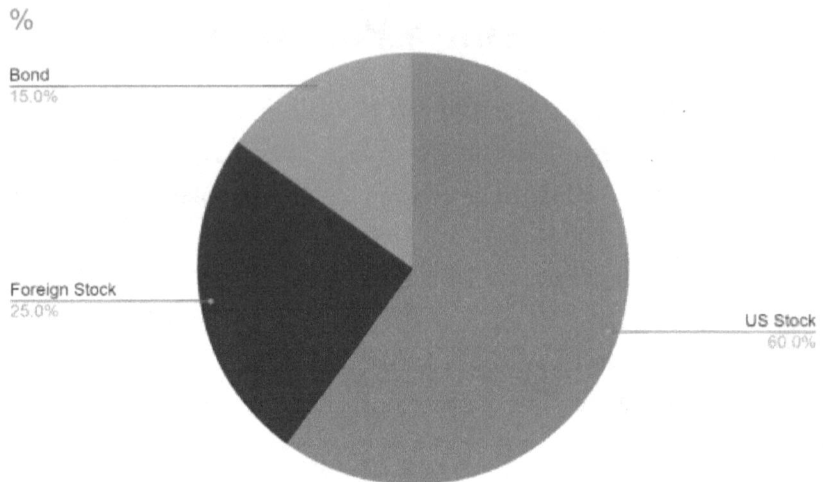

The whole point of showing you how to build a portfolio is not to show you what stocks are good to buy and more about how you can use index funds and ETFs to achieve stable returns and still beat the market most of the time without constantly looking for the next best investment in an individual stock and catching a hype.

The strategy I use is called sector rotation. Combining index investing with a sector rotation strategy will help you to build good habits and understand the market. Building a portfolio suited for index investing requires a few more terms and principles. The easiest thing you can do is to put your money into an index fund. Index investing requires little to no effort on your end as long as you stay the course you will ride the stock market's average return and make this choice a decent investment, However, you are missing out on a lot of potential upsides by being so lazy. Later I will explain how you can use a sector rotation strategy to use in your portfolio that works for you. But first the basics.

If you decide to invest in an index fund or funds that offer little to no fees for index funds or index ETFs, if you just want to invest your money and forget about it you can do that and your index investment will do fairly well. To do so you will need to open a brokerage account. Here I suggest you take advantage of the options your country offers. In Canada, there is something called a TFSA (tax-free savings account). The US equivalent would be an RRSP. If you are not from the US or Canada find the closest thing available to you in your country. Your bank and online brokers offer you to open one of these accounts. Now you can start preparing for your retirement and invest in a variety of different assets through your broker. The benefit of opening a TFSA as early as possible is that the earlier you start your investments will have more time to compound.

Compounding interest is your friend and the earlier you start the better. As the name implies the gains you make through your TFSA are tax-free. I would not use the account meant for your retirement to make silly trades in silly investments you don't understand. If you want to day trade and make a quick buck, open a personal account and pay your taxes accordingly. If the CRA sees unusual high activity on your TFSA they will flag your account and you ruin this great opportunity. First, you should work on your strategy and create a portfolio that will grow and compound realistically for your benefit later in life. Max out the TFSA as early as possible and try to invest every year the amount of your allowed contribution limit. Don't gamble, be serious.

Getting into the habit of investing at 20-50% of what is left for you to live will be one of the habits that will set you free later in life. We as humans are designed to adjust to our environment and repeat the things that work. Self-motivation is a lie, What you have to do if you want to get rid of your bad habits is to change your environment accordingly to welcome new habits that are beneficial to you later in life. Doing what you feel like at any given time purely following your desire is a recipe for failure. Investing and getting wealthy is a mindset you have to acquire with constant change in your behavior.

You want to lose weight but you have the habit of snacking? Look what is in your fridge. Is it sugary snacks? Get rid of them and replace them with something healthy. You're depressed and cannot keep up with cleaning the house and it's always dirty? Throw out everything you are not using and that is just in the way. Have too many different pots, cutlery, and plates enough for ten but you are living alone? Get rid of it and only use the bare minimum of what is needed. You will quickly find out how much cleaner and organized your environment will be and how your unhealthy habits will change to your favor just because you changed the environment around you.

Now you unconsciously adjust to that new environment and are (forced) to change your old destructive behaviors with better ones. The next thing you could be doing is taking advantage of retirement plans through your employer. In Canada that can be done through an RRSP and in the US with a 401K. Talk to your employer to set up one of these investment accounts and decide what that money goes towards every paycheck.

With the TFSA and RRSP you don't want to only put money in it you have to decide on what to invest. The benefit of setting up an RRSP or 401K is that they are tax-deferred. Meaning as long as you don't touch that account until you retire you will not pay taxes. You pay when you withdraw. Money towards these retirement plans will come off your paycheck (before taxes) automatically. If you don't want to manage your own investments what you could do instead is you could also hire someone to manage your investments and see how that person performs in comparison to your index investment. if the investment manager beats the market great you don't have to do anything, just invest in a mutual or hedge fund. However, investing in yourself is not as difficult as many people might think. First of all, I want to introduce the economy in general. To understand the business cycle I like to look at the different phases of the economy the same way I look at the seasons in a year.

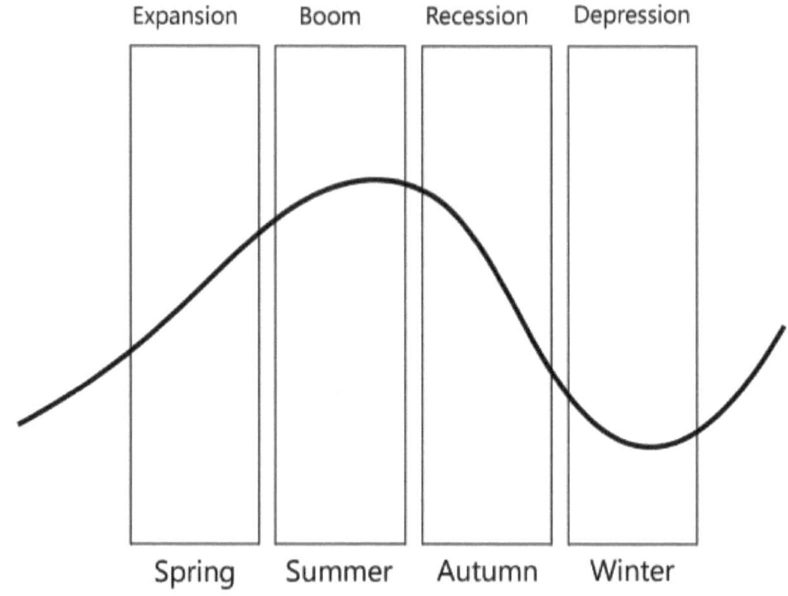

The economy goes through the same cycle every 4-7 years, sometimes even 10 years. Some sectors perform better at different points of the cycle. If you read the cycle just like you read the seasons you can make accurate predictions of what sectors are most likely to outperform other sectors at any given point in the cycle. I will go into more detail about a sector rotation strategy and how to read it later. For now, I want you to imagine you are a farmer. And each season another vegetable will grow which you can harvest. Let's say we are in spring. You plant corn to harvest it in summer and you plant (invest) into pumpkins in the summer to harvest them (Sell High) in Autumn.

Now, look at it from a business perspective. What season do you expect Ice Cream sales to go up? Summer. How about Kites? Well, Autumn. Flower pots in spring and all sorts of gifts on Christmas. Just like you know ahead of time what will sell well next season, you can apply the same principle in buying shares and investing in specific sectors in the economy. If you bought ice cream company stocks in spring and sold them in summer and you bought toy company stocks in autumn to sell them in winter. Congratulations you are using the strategy called sector rotation. If we look at the economic cycle we can see that certain sectors perform better and worse depending on which point of the cycle we find ourselves in. First, long-term let's go through the cycle to understand it better.

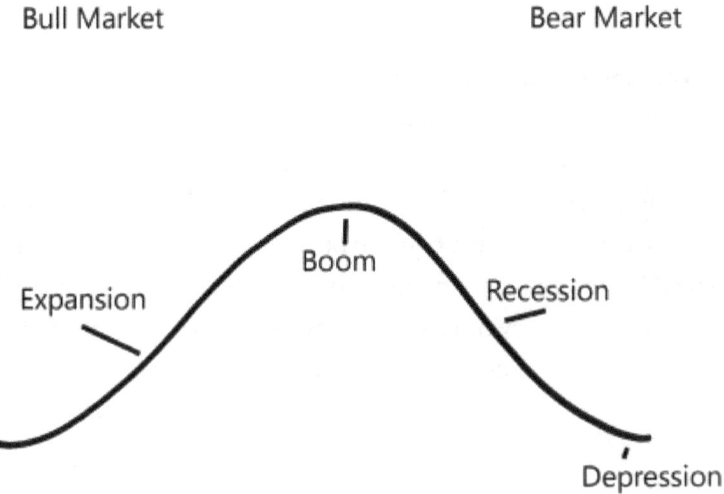

Bull Market

Expansion- is the phase of rapid growth. Industries doing well in this phase are Technologies, Manufacturing and machinery, and basic materials companies processing raw materials(Mining, Wood, Chemicals, etc... in this phase keep your technology stocks and don't sell them because they might still grow. Boom - This is where the rich people sell and the poor people buy. The industries doing well here are. Energy, Oil, solar wind, etc... including staple goods imagine what people need to eat and drink every day.

Bear Market

Recession - Here again, energy and more importantly consumer goods, basic everyday things people need. Food, Utilities, etc, and very important Healthcare. Because even if the economy is doing bad people still need food, electricity, and medicine. Depression - this is the phase when the economy is just coming out of a recession. The industries doing well in this phase are finance(Banks) Technology and Cyclicals(basically non-necessary or luxury goods and services.) Examples: retail, clothes, media, Cars, etc...

You have to understand that the economic cycles every 4-10 years, sometimes the stock market can recover and the economy is still in a recession. That is because the stock market compared to GDP is forward-looking. When investors put their money into the stock market they are doing so because they expect it to go up in the near future. Don't base the cycle on the overall recession when everything is going up you are now in a bull market. The recovery started for the stocks even if the recession is still ongoing in the general economy.

So if you know in what phase the economy is, you now know when to buy and sell. If you are just starting and you missed a buying or selling opportunity, don't worry about selling anything yet until the market loops back around. The number one strategy to make money in the market is to buy low and sell high. If you have good investments building toward your retirement the best thing to do is to buy and hold. You only lose money if you sell. Especially when you panic sell! so don't just sell because everyone else is. Make sure you invest in things you understand and stay the course.

Otherwise don't buy! A bad investor focuses on what gains he can make in the short run. And acts emotionally when things go out of hand. A good investor looks at the risk and how much he or she could potentially lose. You invest when you are sure about it and plan to hold it for a long time based on the fundamentals and growth potential. If you Invest in that manner you simply don't care what your investment does in the short run and you stay the course.

When things go down you buy more, when things go up you buy less but you always keep buying until you reach your goal. We Invest and not trade for a short gain. To get back to what I said earlier about index funds, if you want you could put your money into an index fund that tracks the S&P 500 and forget about it, it will do just fine. But you know that you will miss out on potential upsides for your investments.

There are different types of investments you can make. The easiest way is to buy a tiny share of a company directly off of the stock exchange. Do you want to own a share of your favorite company? Sure, go ahead you can do that by buying a stock without any additional fees like you would have in a mutual fund. The disadvantage of owning individual stocks is that you are most likely not gonna have enough money to be properly diversified. On top of that, you will need to be knowledgeable about each company.

Mutual funds have managers and specialists that are specialized in a specific market sector. I doubt that you can keep up with all your stocks and perform better consistently over several years than professionals who do it as their job. It is possible if you keep the number of investments low and focus your attention on a few companies.

If you like to keep up with everything they do and have a part-time job doing so you can buy good companies for good prices. However, the average person cannot keep up their investments and consistently outperform the market. Keep in mind this is your hard-earned money and you want to succeed, at least in the long run. Only buy individual stocks from companies because you want to own stock in that individual company and you have enough knowledge and understanding. about that company, you want to own a piece of.

If you want to invest and diversify properly into specific sectors, owning individual stocks from that sector is not going to bring you far. Having a solid portfolio with a solid long-term and goal-oriented strategy will bring you further than anything else. especially in the beginning when you are new and while you are learning the basics. Once you understand the market and your strategy enough you can still make small trades here and then or invest in companies you truly believe in. Just don't jeopardize your precious portfolio and savings.

Mutual Funds

A mutual fund is a pool of money from different investors that together achieve more than an individual investor could. Those funds are run by a fund manager who chooses what type of sector to invest in. The advantage here is that you can own a relative % of an entire diversified portfolio which allows you to have a stake in hundreds or thousands of companies for just a fraction of the price instead of trying to own those yourself. It is also cheaper to pay the professionals running a mutual fund than hiring a money investment manager. The disadvantage here is that you still have to pay a fee for the fund managers which is usually 1% but can be higher. If you want to learn about mutual funds almost all brokers offer those, Start by simply going to your local bank and ask an advisor, see what they have to offer.

Index Funds

Index funds are also mutual funds but they have stable assets (like we saw in the graph S&P 500) that's why they are so cheap because they can be predicted by a computer and don't need a human being to manage the fund. ETFs Another option you have is ETFs or exchange-traded funds which are a basket of stocks that you can buy from the stock exchange directly without paying a managing company first. they also do not have any additional fees. ETFs work best for stable assets like large-cap companies or stable sectors that don't require active management. Mutual funds work best for volatile assets that require research and active management.

Earlier we talked about some example portfolios that you can build around your risk tolerance. High-risk High return Low-risk low return. To measure the risks of your portfolio you can use a simple formula that will give you the (Beta) of your portfolio. The Beta is a measure of risk and volatility. It measures how volatile the stock is compared to the market as a whole.

A portfolio with a beta of 1 is as volatile as the market as a whole. more than 1 means more volatile and less than 1 means less volatile. Imagine yourself on a boat with waves on the ocean. High waves high risk but high return low waves are calmer and more stable but less return. The 10-year average beta of a conservative portfolio should give you a return of around 6% per year. Meaning a Beta of 0.6. If you want to earn 7-8% per year your beta would be 0.7 - 0.8. An aggressive portfolio should have a 10% return with a beta between 1 and 1.15 or higher. Imagine your portfolio in a recession. Let's say it took stock prices about 5 years to recover to pre-recession prices. That means with a beta of 1 it would take 5 years for your portfolio to recover.

With a beta of 1.5 only 2-3 years. You have to decide if you want to recover quickly but have higher volatility thus more risk or if you want to make money in the long run and recover slower with less risk. For long-term investing you could also measure the performance of your portfolio on a benchmark like the S&P 500. You can do so by looking at the alpha of your portfolio. The alpha compares your investment portfolio with a benchmark. If you have a negative alpha you underperformed the overall market on that year. If you have a positive alpha you outperform the overall market.

What about the basic language to build a well-diversified portfolio? Small-cap, large-cap growth stocks sectors and indexes what do all these terms mean? It is important to know some simple terms before you can build a good portfolio. When choosing ETFs and Index funds you want to look into stable companies that either have great value or great growth potential or both.

Large-cap stocks are corporations that have a market capitalization of 10 billion or more. Large-cap growth is mainly the tech industry or any other industry that saw rapid growth in a small period. Or see rapid growth whenever the economy cycles back to a recovery and boom phase. Think of companies that deliver from the internet within days. Companies that shaped our way of life with their products and services.

Large Cap Value stocks are also large companies that have seen rapid growth in the past but do not offer much growth anymore. The excess cash those companies have is given back to investors in the form of dividends. That is why they are also called dividend stocks. They switch from rapid growth to being stable with stable returns. Mainly Financials like banks or large holding companies and Consumer-related companies that sell products that are needed no matter what (think of toilet paper, basic food, basic needs).

Mid-cap companies are all companies with a market capitalization under 10 Billion but not less than 2 Billion. The great thing about Mid-cap companies is that they are not as volatile anymore as small-cap companies and still have the potential to grow enormously since they outgrew small-cap status. Large-cap companies see very small growth where you buy your groceries, big chain restaurants, etc. Ask yourself how much bigger can they still get? Think of Mid-cap companies as the younger versions of big companies that do not grow much more in terms of more facilities or products sold. Look for stable growth and promising value. Mid-cap companies are still a good choice when looking for good ETFs. You don't want to miss out on the opportunity of one of them exploding.

Small-cap stocks are all companies under 2 Billion market capitalization. These stocks are not a good idea to buy as ETFs since they are very volatile and unpredictable. This is why they should be actively managed by a mutual fund or by yourself if you have small companies in mind that might make it in the future! Everything smaller is micro-cap stocks and I would not even touch them.

Penny stocks are rarely a good idea except if you work very hard with an intense focus on all current trends surrounding these stocks.

Once you hear a penny stock growing 200% it is probably too late for you to hop in. Please don't make that mistake, unless you want to gamble. How about indexes and sectors? An index measures the movement of a variety of companies from different sectors in the economy. The S&P 500 index for example tracks the top 500 companies in the US. That is why an ETF tracking a specific index is called an index fund. A sector is for example Healthcare or energy. Companies that you can categorize into a specific sector of the economy. Apple would be Tech, ExxonMobil would be energy(Oil) a company looking for a new vaccine would be healthcare, etc... Let's take what we learned and applied it to build an aggressive portfolio.

50% large-cap stocks

25% Mid-cap stock

20% small-cap

5% cash

50% of your portfolio is in large caps and we know large caps are typically more stable than small companies. Small caps are very volatile and I would try to avoid having them as an ETF. it's better if your small caps are managed actively by either you or a mutual fund. Large, mid, and small caps in your portfolio are a great base to start. We can go further and split the large-cap part (half our portfolio) Into Growth and Value ETFs. After working out the fine details you would end up with something like this:

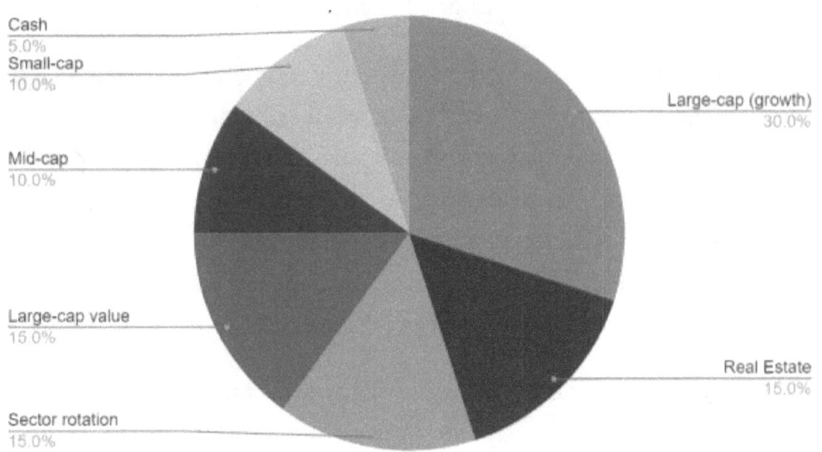

30% Large-cap (growth)

15% Real Estate

15% Sector rotation

15% Large-cap value

10% Mid-cap

10% Small-cap

5% Cash

If you are a beginner the best thing to do is to simply invest in an S&P 500 low fee index fund regularly, that's it. You will perform as good or better than 90% of investors. Someone who knows what he/she is doing to give you a better return will probably charge you a pretty high fee (Mutual fund) making it almost not worth it or not worth it at all. Doing it yourself, especially sector rotating, you need to know what you are doing, otherwise, you will cause more harm than good. I suggest starting simple, getting into the mindset while investing into a low fee US index that tracks a large number of the best-performing companies.

When you learn more and get more confident you may introduce mid and small-cap companies. Only if you are sure of what you are doing you may allocate a small percentage of your portfolio towards sector rotation. The real estate part is built with dividend returns in mind. If you don't want to be diversified into real estate for the long run you could switch real estate with value ETFs with great dividend returns. Value ETFs most of the time already consists of REITs (real estate) at least to some degree.

This portfolio is a simplified example of a combination of index investing and sector rotation. You will have some stability and stable returns in the form of dividends with your Real Estate Investment Trusts (REITs) as well as your Large-cap Value investments. At the same time, you are not missing out on growth and exposure to smaller businesses with growth potential. Alternatively, you could increase the percentage you use in your portfolio for sector rotation.

The percentage of cash and what assets you are invested in will fluctuate over time depending on your investing needs. The possibilities are endless and it all depends on you, your strategy, and risk tolerance. The whole point is to give you simple examples that start with Index investing and combine it with a sector rotation strategy once you are more comfortable with investing regularly into Index funds. When investing there are certain things I look for before deciding to buy. First of all, I try to stay away from individual stocks as they are very volatile and I don't like the idea of going all-in on a single company. Companies go bankrupt, they can tweak numbers easily to hide expenses and before I decide to buy I ask myself will this be still a thing in 10-20 years? Ask yourself what is the future of these companies? and make your own decision. What I am looking for are ETFs and Index funds specifically giving me exposure to a large number of companies and sectors in the economy. I use the S&P 500 as a benchmark or point of reference when analyzing an ETF. There are two main things I am interested in:

1. The 10-year average return compared to my benchmark (S&P 500)

2. A good beta preferably lower than one

If these two things are correct it is most definitely a buy! Because that means that that product outperformed the overall market and is less volatile at the same time. There is not one single magical asset that will outperform the market consistently. That task is on you and your strategy.

Take a deep look at your options and decide for yourself where the best place is for your money to grow. In the next section, I will show you how to combine your index investing with a sector rotation strategy. Many investors make the mistake of not thinking in the long term about their investments and when the share price drops they lose confidence in the share and sell. You only lose money if you sell! That doesn't mean that you hold onto bad investments forever. You want to make sure that what you invest in will give you value in the future. It's all about the mindset.

If you invest periodically every month into companies you are already sure about. You simply don't care what the share price does tomorrow in a month from now. All you care about is your quarterly statement and you adjust your portfolio accordingly because you know in the long run it will grow no matter what. Here are some tips of strategies I use when investing: The simplest strategy is the same as discussed earlier, dollar-cost averaging and investing in lump sums. Meaning when prices are high you buy less. When prices are low you buy more. But you never stop buying, periodically, every month. Investing is a marathon and not a sprint. It requires patience and persistence. You could undergo a little test with yourself. I want you to take out 1K in cash and put it in your wallet. Carry it around and have it with you all the time but no matter what happens, do not spend it! If you have the self-control to walk around with that much money for a long period and not spend it. You are in a good position to start investing and taking your life into your own hands. I want to do a recap for you since it is very important to know this. Dollar-cost averaging is you investing your money into the same investments in intervals (every-month) meaning when an Investment loses value you simply buy more of that asset to lower the average. If you Invest 100$ in 10 shares and the value of your 10 shares drop to 50$. Most people would just sell at a loss... because they act emotionally and see what everyone else is doing. What you should be doing is to take advantage of the situation and buy 10 more shares. Now you own 20 shares for 150$. If the price goes back up to 100 you made 50$ or 25% on your investment by just being consistent. If you are very confident about a particular investment you can try one more strategy.

Let's say you buy shares worth 200$ and you are unsure if it will go up or down so you want to manage your risk (assuming you are already using strategy one). Now you are very lucky and your shares go up to 600$... most people would simply pour more money into the investment because again they act emotionally and greed took them over. What you do instead is you cash out the 200$ you originally invested and keep 400$ in the game. That way you didn't lose any money! And you have twice as much in the game. The most important one is that you stay calm and don't act based on your emotions. You need to understand that these are just tips on how you plan your trades and minimize your risk on certain investments. I want to show you how to invest and what it means to do so every month. Short-term gains and quick money through trades here and there are nothing in comparison to a long-term investing strategy. In the long run, the long-term investors will have the last laugh.

Sector rotation

In the previous chapter, we built a simple portfolio using a sector rotation strategy. Here I want to go into more depth about this strategy so you can use the business cycle and the movement of the markets to your advantage. You might have heard many individuals that simply investing in one index fund is the way to go. But as you know now, you would only move with the market. This is fine if you want to go with the flow. You can do better by focusing a percentage of your portfolio on the sectors in the economy. This strategy should be using 15-20% of your portfolio that you dedicate to specific sectors of the economy at a certain point in the business cycle. The sector rotation strategy has nothing to do with the actual seasons in a year but rather reading the economic cycle just like you would read the seasons.

I want to explain it to you again so you understand. I like to look at the business cycle the same way I look at the seasons. Both are going through the same phases, every time in the cycle. Based on the ever occurring same sequence you can make accurate predictions about what sectors would perform better at any given point in the cycle. Remember the example where you are the farmer preparing crops in one season to sell them in the next? You can apply the same principle to the economy and use Sectors as your crops, the seasons as the business cycle, and the harvest to sell high.

The cycle is not always as smooth as in the illustration. Sometimes you have a cold Summer. Sometimes you have to harvest your crops early because of a very short winter. You can never know. But you always know that one season follows another. In the market, you have to only focus on buying low and selling high. If you missed an opportunity in a particular phase of the cycle that's fine. You can always wait for the market to fully cycle back and then sell. Let's take this simple example of harvesting crops and apply it to the market and its sectors. A sector refers to a group of stocks representing companies focused on a specific sector of the economy. Here are the main categories you should understand.

Financials - Mainly banks, Insurance companies, Mutual funds, and credit unions also count. Real-Estate - Well basically everything involved in the housing market and real estate investment trusts (REITs)

Consumer Discretionary - Non-essential, Luxury goods and services. Think of the Hotel industry, Media production, Automotives, textiles, etc...

Technology - Software, Technology, and services related to tech.

Industrials - Transportation Services Like Airlines, Construction, Manufacturing of products, etc.

Materials - Commodity-related products, Mining, Metals, Chemicals, Forestry, etc.

Consumer staples - Production and distribution of food, beverages. Everyday consumer goods and things people will always need. That includes food and drug retailers and superstores.

Health care - Companies involved in research and manufacturing healthcare-related products. Energy - Oil and gas production.

Communication Services - Cellular, Wireless, and other communication services.

Utilities - Production and distribution of power. Electric, Hydro, and Gas. (somewhat related to the energy sector)

If you want success in picking the right investment. Sectors are an important consideration. Because Different sectors will behave differently based on the economic circumstances. Global and local economical events can affect sectors directly. In a global pandemic and worldwide shutdowns, you can expect the industrial sector to suffer. But benefiting the consumer staples and healthcare sector. Lower interest rates mean more people will borrow money and invest in real estate meaning the financial and real estate sector benefit.

If the oil price drops you can expect that the energy sector will have less revenue and lose money. Therefore every industry dealing with oil and gas is directly affected. If you understand the sectors you will understand the market. You understand the market, you will understand an additional layer to your investments and be able to make better judgments and choices. Over time, an economy goes through periods of growth and contraction. An economy in an expansion, benefits cyclical sectors providing luxury non-essential items. While in an economy that goes through a contraction, non-cyclical or essential goods and services perform better. No stock is immune to an economic downturn. But you as an investor can shift assets from one sector to another depending on the business cycle.

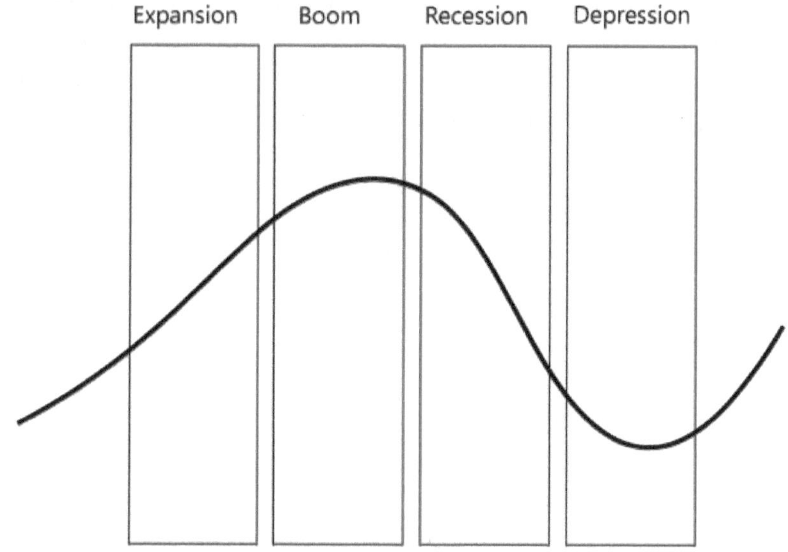

It is not wise to predict the market or even worse trying to time it. What we do know is that the economic cycle is a natural occurrence that happens in the same sequence. It takes about 4-7 years, sometimes longer before it will repeat itself. Keep in mind that a boom can last and the economy can hit a ceiling and stay there for quite a while. The next question you may ask is what sector of the economy does well at what moment in the cycle? The easiest way to know in what phase of the cycle we are in is to look at sector performance in the last quarter and compare it with the present moment. Have a look at the overall market performance and what sectors did well and what sectors did not do well to determine in what phase of the business cycle we are in the present moment. Knowing this is extremely important when investing. It can give you good information on what sectors to focus on. I recommend, sector rotating about 15-20% of my portfolio. You cannot predict the market but the business cycle always moves in the same sequence. Just like the seasons After spring comes summer and after summer comes autumn and winter. When investing with a sector rotation strategy you want to be the farmer who plants corn in the spring so you can harvest it in the summer. You want to buy stocks when they are low in one phase of the economy and sell high in the next phase. The easiest way to read the cycle is by comparing sector performance. Here is an example:

Sectors:	5 Day Mov Avg	20 Day Mov Avg
Financials	59%	81%
Real Estate	63%	82%
Consumer Discretionary	36%	73%
Technology	78%	88%
Industrials	56%	76%
Materials	73%	65%
Consumer Staples	40%	43%
Health Care	61%	60%
Energy	87%	93%
Communication Services	63%	75%
Utilities	25%	35%

We can see that the top-performing sectors are energy, tech, materials. While the worst performing sectors are utilities, consumer discretionary, and consumer staples. So what does that mean? Let's compare it to the business cycle and what sectors perform well in what phase of the cycle.

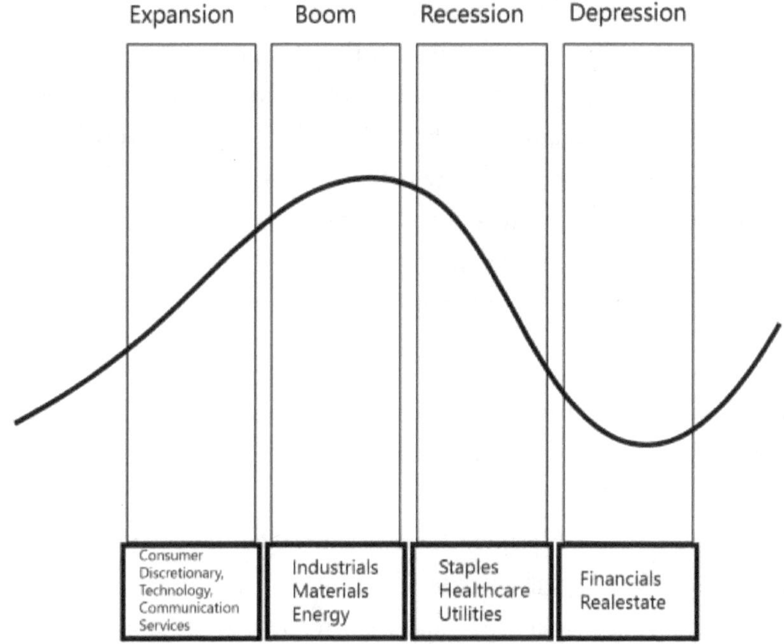

On this graph, we can see that basic materials and energy tend to perform best in a late bull phase but the data also shows the technology sector is still being strong and basic materials just started to do well.

If we compare the cycle to the seasons. Spring, summer, autumn, and winter. We can see that we are between spring and summer or between the late phase of an expansion and the early phase of a boom. You are the farmer and you want to sell your crops when they are grown and prepare to plant other crops that will grow in the next season. As an investor that means that in this example you are selling your materials and energy high and buying consumer staples, healthcare, and Utilities low. Well, you might ask yourself, why is that? The worst performing sector in this example by far are utilities and consumer staples. You are right. What most people do band most gurus try to sell you is to buy high and sell higher. That is not how to make money. You make money by buying low and selling high. The beauty of sector rotation is that it never skips a phase. The cycle is always the same, helping you to prepare and make better decisions compared to only going for the next hot thing. Sometimes you might be stuck in one phase for a year and sometimes the market goes through two phases in only 3 months. You can never know that, but what we do know is that the market never skips a phase and plays out in the same sequence, every time. Now that we know the movement of the market and that different sectors tend to perform better with each phase of the economic cycle. How would our strategy look in practice?

Here is a table I made and use to sector rotate my investments. Based on historical data and sector performance we can have an approximate ideal time to buy and sell:

Sectors:	Expansion	Boom	Recession	Depression
Financials	Sell	buy	Buy (Low)	Sell (High)
Real Estate	Sell	Buy	Buy (Low)	Sell (High)
Consumer Discretionary	Sell (High)	Sell	Buy	Buy (Low)
Technology	Sell (High)	Sell	Buy	Buy (Low)
Industrials	Buy (Low)	Sell (High)	buy	Buy
Materials	Buy (Low)	Sell (High)	Sell	Buy
Consumer Staples	Buy	Buy (Low)	Sell (High)	Sell
Health Care	Buy	Buy (Low)	Sell (High)	Sell
Energy	Buy (Low)	Sell (High)	Sell	Buy
Communication Services	Sell (High)	Sell	Buy	Buy (Low)
Utilities	Buy	Buy (Low)	Sell (High)	Sell

The colored fields stating Sell (High) and Buy (Low) indicate a strong correlation with the actual performance of the sector. The non-colored fields are a suggestion but do not indicate a strong correlation and enough evidence for a good time to buy or sell. You have to make your judgment based on sector performance. Sell indicates better performance while Buy Indicates a weaker performance of a specific sector. You want to buy low and sell high. The entire table is for you as guidance but does not always play out in the exact chronological order for each cycle. Sometimes the market contracts rapidly or a phase takes longer than usual but the market will never skip a phase in the cycle.

No sector is 100% save against a rapid market correction. The stock market is not the economy. You should not ignore changes in the economy and certain events that have an impact on the market. Just like with sectors certain events are directly linked with the markets. Simple action and reaction. A combination of events created from the interaction between the economy, the market, and human psychology. What are some events that are associated with phases of the cycle?

Expansion

In this phase, the economy begins to improve. Spending grows and interest rates are low. The financial sector is still reaping the benefits of lowering interest rates and it might be a good time to sell. The technology, communications, and consumer discretionary sector are more likely to outperform other sectors in this phase.

Boom

The improving economy slowly reaches an end as interest rates begin to rise rapidly again. A flood of IPOs, craze in the market of buying extremely overvalued stocks and your neighbor who does even know what day of the week it is suddenly talking about investing are usually good indicators that we are in a boom. At this stage, you want to be fearful because others are greedy. The energy, materials, and utility sectors perform better at this stage.

Recession

In this phase, the economy begins to slow after seeing rapid growth. The best indicator you can use to see if an economy is expanding or contracting is to look at real GDP. Consumers and investors are not confident anymore. Euphoria ends and fear starts. The fear and worst consumer expectations in the cycle combined with interest rates at their highest point for that cycle, lead to a decline in industrial production and spending on non-essential goods. This is the time where Consumer Staples (essential goods) Healthcare and Utilities perform the best. Financials and real estate perform the worst.

Depression

The economic bottom of a cycle. Production is low and GDP is contracting. Interest rates slowly begin to rise again and consumer expectations are getting better. In this phase of the cycle, tech is slowly rising again after being on a massive discount. As interest rates begin to fall the financial sector benefits and improves. People slowly gain back confidence to spend money on real estate and consumer discretionary products such as retail and car manufacturers. The stock market is not the economy! The stock market is forward-looking and you shouldn't ignore what is going on in the actual economy when investing. If you want to only check in what phase of the economic cycle we are to determine what sectors to buy and sell. You can look at the sector's overall performance and adjust accordingly. If for example energy is doing increasingly better since the last quarter. That would be a strong indicator that we are in a late Bull (boom) phase or Summer. To determine the phase of the actual economy you have to look at different factors. Look at Real GDP, The Consumer confidence index, Unemployment rates, and the stock market.

The most important factor in my opinion is real GDP as real Gross Domestic Production is inflation-adjusted. For the stock market specifically, you should watch interest rates closely. Since interest rates are the first things to change to control spending in a country. In times of a crisis like we had with Covid in 2020. Governments print money to inflate markets and lower interest rates to increase consumer spending. Unemployment rates as compared to the past few years are also a good indicator to see in what condition the economy of a country is. The stock market is forward-looking. As investors buy and sell based on their own perceived future. In a way, the stock market is a good indicator of what is about to come soon. For you, as an investor, the idea is to be ahead of the game each season meaning to prepare the crops (sectors) this season to harvest (sell) the crops you prepared last season now.

For example, if we would be in between summer and autumn, the sector for autumn will be a good buy and the sector for winter will be even better. Hold onto them and sell when high the next season! Sector rotation should only be around 15% -20% of your portfolio. The rest should consist of assets that will give you value in the future and a stable return. But Hey, how you invest and allocate your portfolio is totally up to you. As discussed earlier the movement of the stock market is different from the movement of the actual economy in a country. Not completely unrelated but rather one is a precursor to the other. Not only is the stock market forward looking in comparison to other measures of the economy like GDP. but is mainly driven by emotions and people's perception of the economy. You must look at a variety of factors to determine if investment for the long term into a specific sector is beneficial to you or not. You should also be aware of the psychology of the stock market.

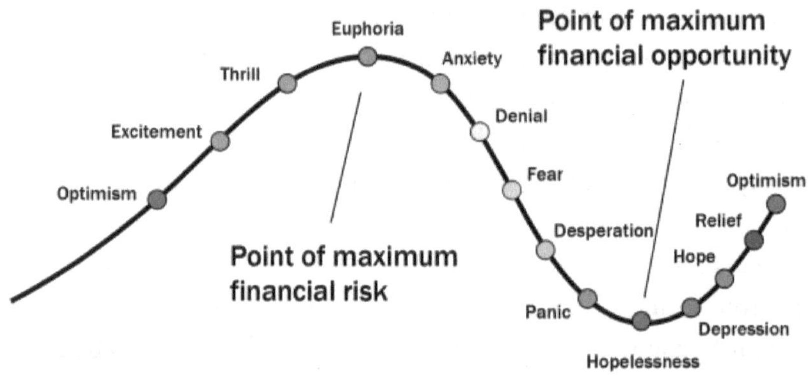

In the early phase of a bull market Optimism rises and investors start to get confident. As the Bear market reaches the top, suddenly everyone is a genius investor. People you deal with every day are suddenly talking about their first investments. More companies decide to go public. There is a craze in the market and everyone has the fear of missing out (FOMO). The top of a bull market is the point where successful investors experience the highest possible risk in the cycle.

As the markets enter a recession there is denial. Bad investors start to regret their decisions and do not possess the patience nor the knowledge to deal with a falling market. While the only thing you have to do to be a successful investor is to buy low, sell high. Fomo is the exact opposite, it is buying high and selling low. Anyone asking you: "what is the secret to your investing?" If you told them: "I buy low and sell high." they would answer: "I already know that. So why are you buying an asset that went up incredibly fast without any fundamentals backing it up?" Ultimately the market's trajectory is determined by two emotions, greed and fear. Investing is a skill.

Unlike other skills where you have a sense of what is right and wrong. Investing successfully cannot be done through your gut feeling. It is emotionless and all emotions do, is getting in the way of your success. As markets reach the bottom of a bear market. Successful investors recognize this as the point of maximum financial opportunity. The big players in the market include big hedge funds. Understand that the market is driven by human emotions. They do not only deploy large amounts of money and hope for their investments to go up or down. Not even technically analyze specific investments. They actively engineer their desired outcomes. If they want a stock to go up. They will pay analysts and professionals to write positively about them before deploying large amounts of money into the stock, driving up the price. Retail investors see this and FOMO driving the price higher (greed). If they want a stock to go down they do the opposite. Writing negative things about them and selling large amounts dropping the price. Retail investors get scared and sell (fear). Now the stock can be shorted. No matter what market, every market is made up of people.

All they have to do is tap into two simple emotions, which are greed and fear. We do things well and we see everyone but us making money, the fear of missing out and greed overcomes us making us buy into things without fundamentally understanding it. When the euphoria ends and there is a big sell-off. We enter a state of denial and eventually sell. If you let your emotions decide your investing behavior you will buy high and sell low. After every market crash, the number of active investors declined significantly.

After losing big, it seems that most people decided that investing is not for them and give up. As time passes and the markets slowly get flooded with active investors again. The market gets overinflated until it crashes again. In a way, it is a self-correcting mechanism. You can see it as a wealth-transfer from the losers to the winners. If you let emotions rule your Investing decisions, you will always lose! We learned how different sectors behave at different phases of the economy, here is a small illustration of the psychological side of things. The secret to successful investing is *shocker* buy low and sell high, sounds so easy right? Easier said than done. Most people simply follow a trend. If they see something shiny going up, they think it is a good idea to blindly follow. In the end, everything will always fall back to its fundamentals. There is a famous quote of Warren Buffett, I want to share:

"Be fearful when others are greedy, and greedy when others are fearful".

When others are greedy, prices typically boil over. When others are fearful, it may present a buying opportunity. You want to look at the entire situation and 99% of the time simply observe. Intelligence is simply making accurate predictions of the future based on the current information available to you. If you do not have an accurate model of reality you will not be able to make accurate predictions benefiting your life.

This applies not only to investing by being knowledgeable about the market and human psychology but is also true for every aspect of your life. Especially your worldview and the way you think about your place in this world. Crashes will always happen, no matter what. It's a cycle. The important thing is how you prepare for such situations. In a market crash, there are four things you can do.

You can choose to do nothing! That's right non-action is also an action and in most cases a better choice than actually doing something. Secondly, you could continue investing as you did anyways. Allocating the same amount of money you always did periodically and staying the course!

Number three, my favorite. When prices are high you buy less, when prices are low you take the opportunity and buy low. Since investments you would buy anyways are now on a massive discount. The only thing you do not do is sell. You simply buy and hold and if the opportunity comes you take it and buy more. This only works for investments you did your due diligence for. Markets always recover, Individual stocks and their companies on the other hand might not.

The last and most popular option, Option four:" Sell". The movement of the market is a reflection of human behavior and psyche. Unfortunately most invest money into things they do not fully understand and end up panic selling! The hype and euphoria do not last forever. Making profits when markets are booming does not make you a genius investor. What makes you a good investor is what you do during bad times. How well you cope and prepare for the moment to shine. You want to invest when everyone else is panicking. The stock markets cycle is an opportunity for people like you and me to make money on assets that are on a massive discount.

While this discount happens for housing prices and other industries sometimes only once or twice in a lifetime. The same opportunity happens for you in the stock market multiple times throughout your life. You absolutely must educate yourself and be prepared with a solid plan and strategy to take advantage of the opportunities present to you in life. Opportunities will always be there, the trick is to be able to see them and take them. Have you ever heard the sentence Past performance is not indicative of future results? Economists and so-called professionals can only look at past events and previous data to predict anything. This happened last time which means it will happen this time too.

Yes, inverted yield curves, Low-interest rates at times of high unemployment might all be signs that occurred before market crashes. Knowing all the data and indicators does not make you a fortune teller. There are simply too many variables and human emotions involved to accurately predict anything. You must be able to tune off the noise, everyone will say something and hope for the things to happen that benefit themselves. Everyone, including yourself. Market corrections and market crashes will always happen. Always! And the market will always recover. It is all about your mindset, patience, and how you decide to ride the wave.

All contents presented in this book have been prepared for informational purposes only, and are not intended to provide, and should not be relied on for any personal investment, tax, or accounting advice. All information mentioned is what worked for me. You should, before making any decision regarding any information, strategies, or product mentioned in this book, consult your own financial or accounting advisors to consider whether the product is appropriate for you, based on your objectives, financial situations, and needs.